"Behold, a throne stood in heaven, with one seated on the throne! And he who sat there appeared like jasper and carnelian, and round the throne was a rainbow that looked like emerald...From the throne issued flashes of lightning, and voices and peals of thunder, and before the throne burnt seven torches of fire, which are the seven spirits of God."

Revelation 4: 2,5

Like this book?

🛒 **Purchase another copy here:**

Australasia: www.store.parousiamedia.com/book

USA: www.parousiausa.com/format/book

✂ **Access a FREE paper craft activity here:**

www.parousiamedia.com/gods-love-in-the-sky-3d-paper-rainbow-prayer-box-activity

Scroll down to the pdf viewer and click "Download here" to access pdf.

Copyright © 2024 Parousia Media Pty Ltd. All rights reserved.

Parousia Media Pty Ltd
PO Box 59
Galston, NSW 2159
parousiamedia.com

Written by Judi Marie Prasser
Illustrated by Alejandro Fernandez-Cotta Andrade

Printed and Distributed by Parousia Media in Australia
ISBN: 978-1-923131-50-7

Dear _____

Know that God's promise to Noah was a promise to you too.

Love from _____

Sometimes there are loud storms in the dark night and they are a bit scary.

Little one, don't worry, you are not alone.

Do you know that God loves you very much?

He promised us He would always look after us.

Little one, do you know how God keeps His promise to us?

With His special painting in the sky.

God comes and pushes the rainclouds

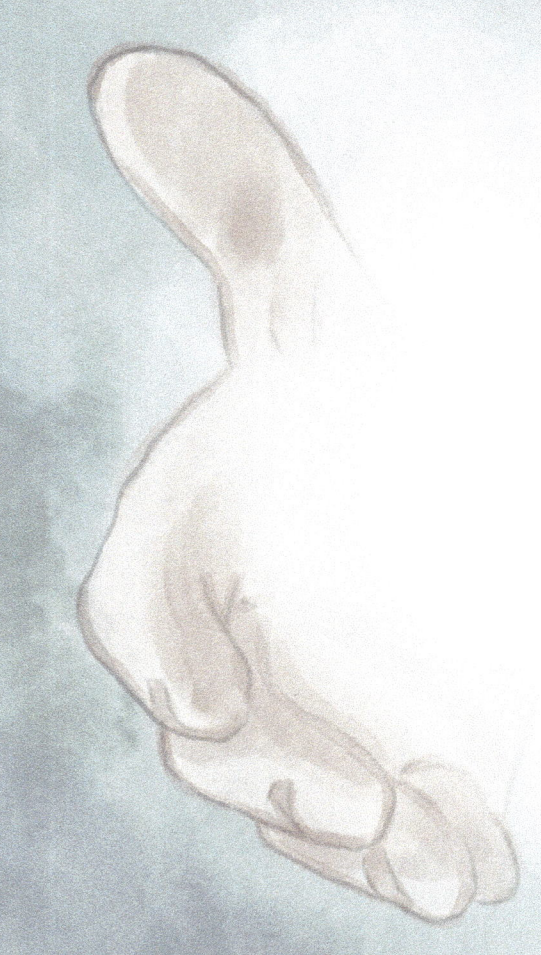

away to make room for His painting.

Then He gets His paintbrush and paints beautiful colours in the sky.

God calls this painting a Rainbow

Little one, do you know what God's favourite number is?

So God put seven colours in His rainbow.

The seven colours of God's rainbow are:

Red

Yellow

Orange

Little one, do you know what God's favourite colour is?

Blue

So God put two different types of blue in His rainbow.

The first blue is a plain blue colour, just like the sky.

The second blue colour is called "Indigo".

Indigo is dark blue and purple mixed together.

Indigo recipe:
2/3 blue
+
1/3 purple

All the other colours are just used one time.

But for the colour blue, God put two.

Little one, whenever we see a rainbow, we know it's true:

God is showing His love for me and you.

A rainbow is ...

Like this book?

🛒 **Purchase another copy here:**

Australasia: www.store.parousiamedia.com/book

USA: www.parousiausa.com/format/book

✂ **Access a FREE paper craft activity here:**

www.parousiamedia.com/gods-love-in-the-sky-3d-paper-rainbow-prayer-box-activity

Scroll down to the pdf viewer and click "Download here" to access pdf.